Y0-AVA-929

SEWING WITH YARN
An Introduction to Sewing by Hand

by Barbara Carmer Schwartz

Photographs by Edward Stevenson

J. B. Lippincott Company/Philadelphia and New York

For Nancy and Betsy

U.S. Library of Congress Cataloging in Publication Data

Schwartz, Barbara Carmer.
  Sewing with yarn: an introduction to sewing by hand.

  Includes index.
  SUMMARY: Introduces sewing with yarn including discussions of materi-
als and yarns and instructions for suggested projects.
  1. Sewing—Juvenile literature. 2. Yarn—Juvenile literature. [1. Sewing. 2.
Yarn. 3. Handicraft] I. Stevenson, Edward. II. Title.
TT712.S38   746.2'1   76-41403
ISBN-0-397-31736-0   ISBN-0-397-31737-9 (pbk.)

CONTENTS

ABOUT SEWING WITH YARN

Sewing with yarn is an easy way to learn about hand sewing. To get started, you need some scraps of fabric and yarn and a large needle.

After you have practiced just a few simple stitches you will be able to make many kinds of clothes and decorations. This skill will often come in handy when you need or want something special. For example, you can make pillows for your room the size, shape, and color you want. Or you can design a Halloween mask with horrible scars. Or you might make a cap to match a jacket.

A group of girls and boys made costumes for a class play using inexpensive cotton fabric and yarn. After the play had been performed, several of the girls remodeled their costumes (using yarn sewing, of course) into halters and drawstring bags. Some of the boys turned their costumes into aprons which they used in wood shop.

Yarn sewing projects can be made quickly. Most of the items in this book can be finished in a few hours. And they may last for years.

Sewing with yarn gives you a chance to use lots of colors and patterns. When you practice new stitches, try several combinations of colors to see what different results you can create. You can also vary the size of the stitches, which will make them look completely different. In fact, everything you sew with yarn will be original, for when two people follow the same directions the results are never quite the same.

After you make a few simple projects which are sewn with yarn, you will find it easy to handle a smaller needle and thread. Then you will be ready to learn how to sew more complicated articles. In the meantime, yarn sewing will be easy, fast, inexpensive, convenient, colorful, creative, and fun.

EQUIPMENT, FABRICS, AND YARNS

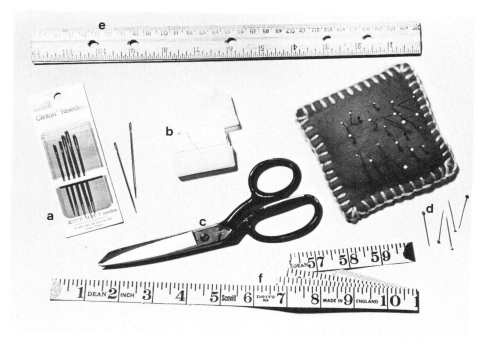

Many of the sewing materials shown above may already be in your home. If not, you can buy them in dime stores, department stores, fabric and needlework shops, and some supermarkets. Small pieces of sewing equipment such as needles and pins are called *notions*. In many stores, you will find notions in a separate section from fabrics or yarns.

Darning needles (a) are large, sharp needles with large eyes. They come in many sizes. For the projects in this book, sizes 14 to 18 are

6

good, depending on the weight of the yarn and fabric used. If you have trouble threading your needle, try one with a larger eye.

Tailor's chalk (b) works better than blackboard chalk or pencils for marking cutting and sewing lines on fabric. Tailor's chalk makes a sharp line and brushes off easily when you are finished. You can buy it in light colors for marking dark fabrics and in dark colors for marking light fabrics.

Cutting shears 7 or 8 inches long (c) are sharp scissors which are used only for cutting fabric.

Straight pins (d) should be sharp. If pins are rusty or bent, throw them away.

A 12-inch ruler (e) is necessary for measuring fabric and for marking where you will sew.

A tape measure (f) is used for measuring parts of your body such as your waist, your hips, or around your head, because it hugs curved surfaces.

Fabric scraps from two sources can be used for yarn sewing projects:
1) Old clothing; old linens (sheets, pillowcases, and towels)
2) Leftover fabric from home sewing projects

Leftover fabric has never been used and may seem more attractive than old clothing or linens. But you will be surprised at the number of good-looking articles you can make from the used stuff. Besides, it is usually lying around the house when you need it for a project. Be sure clothing or linen is no longer being used before you cut it up.

Some sources of used fabric are the legs cut from jeans or other pants, the top and bottom ends of sheets and towels, and the backs of shirts, dresses, pajamas, and robes. These places are often in excellent condition long after holes have appeared elsewhere.

Some good fabrics for yarn sewing are medium-weight denim,

muslin, and cotton flannel. Lightweight broadcloth, gingham, percale, and calico are good for making soft articles such as halters, party aprons, or potholders. If someone gives you a pile of scraps, ask him or her to help you identify them and to select one which will be strong and easy to work with.

Felt is an excellent fabric for some yarn sewing projects. It does not ravel (come apart) at the cut edges. It comes in many beautiful colors. You can buy it by the yard or in small pieces about 9 inches square. It must be dry-cleaned, however, so you will want to use it for articles which will not get dirty quickly.

If you buy a piece of fabric for yarn sewing, check the width before deciding how much you will need to have cut from the bolt. Most cotton fabrics are either 36 or 45 inches wide. Felt, however, is usually 72 inches wide. Ask the salesperson to help you decide how much fabric to buy.

Yarns for sewing may be wool, Orlon or other acrylics, or nylon. Yarn is made by twisting two or more threads together to form a long strand. Two threads form a lightweight yarn (called two-ply yarn). Three or four threads form medium-weight yarns (called three-ply

and four-ply yarns). Both kinds are easy to use. If you know people who knit, crochet, embroider, or work needlepoint, they may be willing to give you small amounts of leftover yarns. The tapestry yarn used in needlepoint is especially suited to yarn sewing.

Stuffing is used in pillows and pincushions. Old nylon pantyhose, stockings, or light-colored nylon socks make fine stuffing. They are lightweight and machine washable. Wash and dry them, then cut them into strips about 1/2 inch wide.

If you live where there are pine or fir trees, collect the needles which have fallen to the ground. You can also use grass clippings from your lawn or a nearby park. Store needles or clippings in a cool, dry place for a few days before using them as stuffing. Sift through them and remove any twigs or pebbles after they are thoroughly dry.

You can also buy polyester fiber filling by the pound at the dime store. Like nylon stockings, it is lightweight and machine washable.

CUTTING OUT PROJECTS

Some projects in this book are started by measuring fabric with a ruler and marking these measurements with chalk. Then the fabric is cut along the chalk lines.

Measure and cut fabrics on a smooth, clean table or counter. A kitchen table or a table with a plastic or linoleum top works well.

Marking Fabric

Before you mark fabric and begin cutting it, look to see how the fabric is woven. Most fabrics are tightly woven of threads so thin you have to look closely to see them. Burlap, however, is loosely woven of coarse threads. The burlap fabric in the photograph (a) shows how threads run from the top to the bottom (called the lengthwise grain) and from one side to the other (crosswise grain). If the fabric is cut straight along these thread lines it will hold its shape.

Burlap is woven in a plain weave, which means that the threads cross over and under other threads without skipping any. Some

a   b

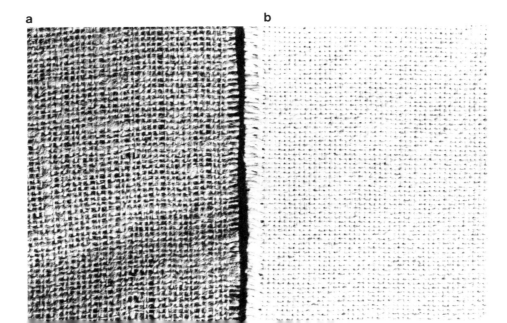

fabrics are woven in patterns which form designs in the cloth. For example, monk's cloth (b) is woven in a basketweave pattern. The threads cross over and under several threads at a time.

When you mark fabric, pay attention to the direction of the threads. For example, mark a practice mat (page 14) so that two sides of the mat follow two lengthwise threads and two sides follow two crosswise threads.

Felt is not a woven fabric. You can cut it in any direction.

Right and Wrong Side

Some fabrics look the same on both sides and some do not. Some have an obvious right side and an obvious wrong side. With others, you will have to decide which is to be the right side and which the wrong. With all fabrics, the right side is the side that shows and the wrong side does not show when the article is completed.

Pinning and Cutting

If the directions for a project call for folding the fabric into two layers before marking it, be sure to pin the layers together. Pins should be spaced about 2 inches apart all the way around the fabric. After you have marked the cutting lines, place more pins *inside* the lines. Then remove the pins from around the edge of the fabric.

Place one hand on the fabric to hold it flat on the table. Hold your shears in the other hand. Cut through the fabric all the way around on the cutting lines. If you are right-handed, cut with these lines to the right of your left hand so that you can see where you are cutting. If you are left-handed, cut with these lines to the left of your right hand.

After cutting, remove the pins.

FOUR SIMPLE STITCHES

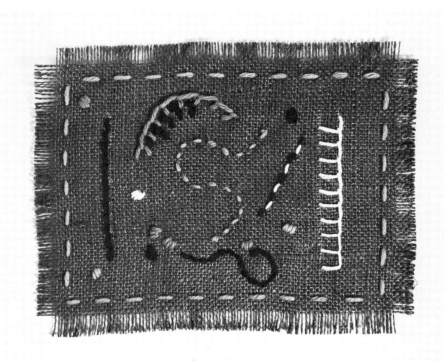

When you are first learning to sew with needle and yarn, it is a good idea to practice stitching on loosely woven fabric. It's easy to push the needle in and out of either burlap or monk's cloth. But whatever type of fabric you decide on, choose one you like. Match it with some yarn that looks good with it. Sewing will be more fun if you choose materials and colors that you like even when you are just practicing.

Cutting a Practice Mat

With ruler and chalk, mark a piece of fabric 8 inches wide and between 8 and 12 inches long. Follow the lengthwise and crosswise threads when you mark. Cut the fabric carefully along the chalk lines.

Next, pull out the first two or three threads all the way around the four cut edges. This will start the fringe and show you whether or not you cut straight. Trim the sides evenly if you see that they are crooked. You should wait to finish the fringe, however, until the stitching is completed.

Threading the Needle

Cut a piece of yarn the length of your arm. It doesn't matter if your arms are long or short. Your arm length will be a good length for you to use.

Thread the darning needle by wrapping one end of the yarn tightly around the needle. Remove the needle. Push the fold through the eye. Pull it through from the other side as shown in the photograph.

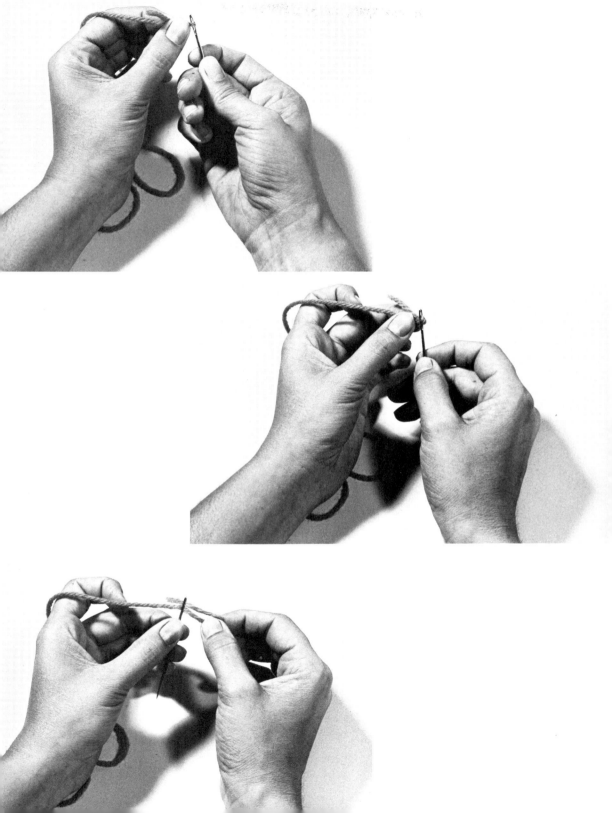

Keep on pulling it until several inches of yarn have slid through the eye to the other side of the needle. This will keep it from pulling out of the needle as you sew.

Knot the longer end of the yarn by forming a loop and pulling the end through it. With practice you can knot the end by rubbing it between your thumb and first finger to form a loop and then pulling the loop down until it tightens.

Hide the knots on the wrong side of the fabric. Then pull all these knots up snug against the underside of the cloth. If the fabric is tightly woven, this is not a problem. If it is loosely woven, a knot may pull right through. To avoid this, hold the knot in place with your thumb and first finger (thumb on the right side, first finger on the wrong side) until several stitches have been made. This will keep the knot from popping through the fabric.

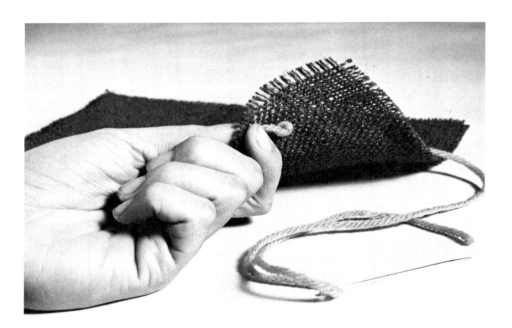

Running Stitch

Running stitches are often used to sew two pieces of fabric together. Sometimes they are part of a design. The wall hanging on page 76 is outlined with running stitches.

To sew running stitches: Guide your needle in and out of the fabric, making stitches that are the same size on both sides of the fabric. You can mark the points where the needle will go in and out with ruler and chalk, to make sure the stitches will all be the same size. Or you may draw a design of curved lines to follow with your needle.

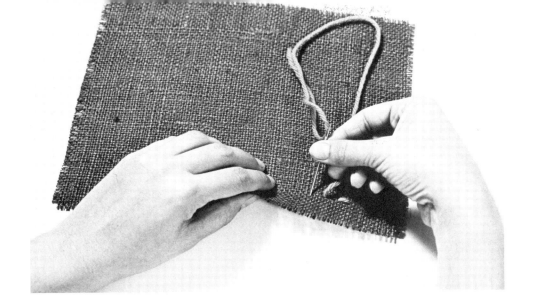

For a smooth line of running stitches, pull the yarn all the way through each time you put the needle through the fabric. Be sure you do not pull the yarn so tight that the fabric draws up into puckers.

After you have learned to sew running stitches evenly, you can put the needle through the fabric more than once before pulling the yarn all the way through.

Sew running stitches on your practice mat about 1 inch inside the edge all the way around. Then try making running stitches in a curved line near the middle of the practice mat.

Tack Stitch

Tack stitches hold the yarn in place at the end of a line of stitches. Each time a piece of yarn is almost used up or a line of stitches is complete, tack the yarn in place by making several tiny stitches one on top of the other on the wrong side of the fabric.

Tack stitches also are used as part of a design on the right side of the fabric. For example, the lion cub pillow on page 46 has eyes made with tack stitches in the center. When they are used in designs, they may be larger than when they are used to end a line of stitches.

To end a line of stitches with tack stitches: Bring the needle through the fabric from the right side to the wrong side. Bring the needle up to the right side just next to where you began. Repeat these steps several times, placing the stitches on top of one another, or very

close to one another. The stitches should be very small. Pick up only one or two threads in the fabric so that the stiches barely show on the right side.

To make decorative tack stitches: Follow the steps for making tack stitches on the wrong side, except that the stitches should be made on the right side and may be 1/4 to 1/2 inch long. End the yarn on the wrong side with tiny tack stitches.

Use tack stitches to end your practice rows of running stitches. Then make as many decorative tack stitches on the right side of the practice mat as you like. Group them together or scatter them; make them long or short. End each group on the wrong side with tiny tack stitches.

Backstitch

Backstitches are often used to sew two pieces of fabric together. They make a stronger seam than running stitches. As a design stitch on the right side of an article, backstitches make attractive solid lines. Their use in the place mat on page 75 is an example.

To sew backstitches: Mark with chalk the line to be stitched. Bring the needle up to the right side of the fabric about 1/4 inch from the end of the line. Bring the needle down to the wrong side at the end of the line (a). Bring it up again to the right side 1/4 inch from where the first stitch began (b). Repeat these steps along the chalk line. Pull the yarn all the way through each time you bring your needle through the fabric so that the stitch will be smooth and even. Try a straight line of backstitches on your practice mat. Then try a curved line.

a

Blanket Stitch

The blanket stitch is often used to finish the edge of an article such as a blanket (which is how it got its name). It makes a fine design stitch in straight or curved lines, either alone or with other stitches.

23

Blanket stitches are also used to sew two pieces of fabric together. Blanket stitching is used in the pillow on page 26.

To sew blanket stitches: Draw two parallel lines about 1/2 inch apart. Bring the needle up to the right side at the end of the lower line. Hold the yarn down with your free thumb. Bring the needle down to the wrong side on the upper line, about 1/4 inch to one side (a). Bring the needle back to the right side on the lower line, directly below (b). Draw the needle through, over the loop of yarn. Repeat

a

b

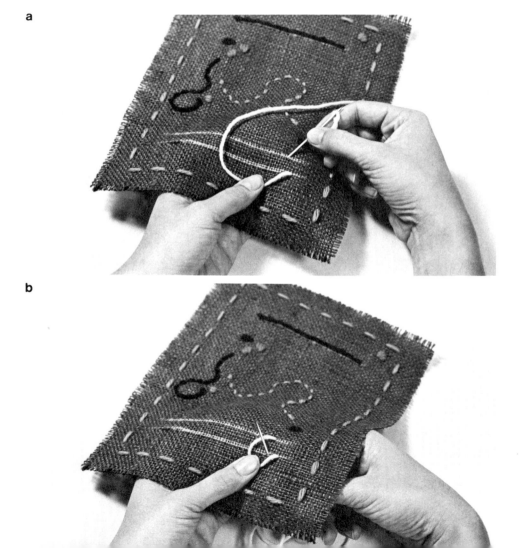

these steps all the way along the lines.

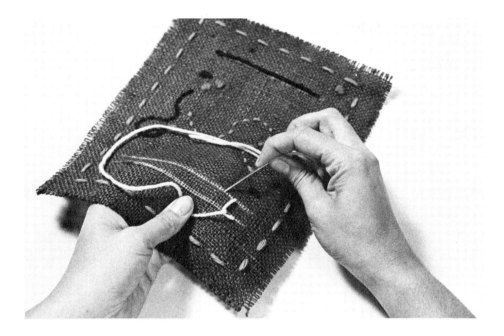

To use blanket stitches to finish an edge, rather than as part of a design, draw a chalk line about 1/2 inch from the edge of the fabric. Bring the needle up to the right side close to the edge. Follow the steps for blanket stitching above, using the edge as the lower line.

Try some blanket stitches between parallel lines, straight and curved, on your practice mat.

Finishing the Practice Mat

After you have practiced stitching over a square or rectangle of fabric, finish fringing the edges by pulling out more threads. Use it as a table or dresser mat in your bedroom. Don't plan on giving this mat away as a gift. It is a practice project, and some of your first stitches may look a bit crooked. But your sewing will improve — with practice.

PILLOWS

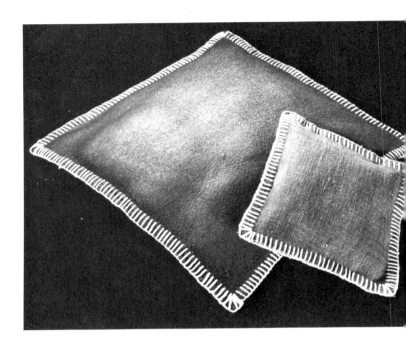

Square Pillows

TYPE OF FABRIC	Denim, muslin, chintz, quilted cotton, gingham, or felt
SIZE OF FABRIC	9 inches by 18 inches
YARN	4 or 5 arm lengths
STUFFING	See page 9 for suggestions

Cutting the Fabric

Measure the fabric with a ruler and chalk. Be sure to mark along a lengthwise thread and a crosswise thread. Cut carefully on the chalk lines.

Sewing the Pillow Together

Fold the fabric in half, right sides facing out, so that it forms two layers 9 inches by 9 inches. Pin it about 1 inch from the edges all the way around.

Sew around three sides of the pillow with blanket stitches. Leave the fourth side open.

Remove the pins from all four sides.

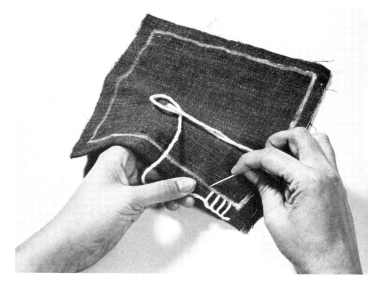

Stuffing the Pillow

Stuff the pillow, using your fingers or the blunt end of a pencil to reach the corners. Stuff the far corners first. Continue stuffing until the pillow feels firm but not hard.

Pin the open end closed. Sew it with blanket stitches.

More Pillows

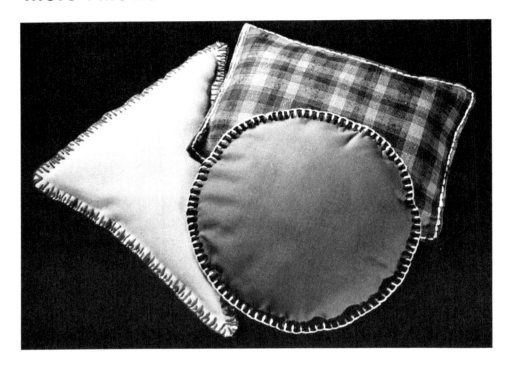

After you have made a pillow or two, you may want to make some larger pillows. Any size up to 24 inches by 24 inches makes sense. Remember, the larger the pillow, the longer it takes to sew and the more fabric and stuffing are needed.

Pillows do not have to be square, of course. They can be round. Or they can be the shape of long rectangles, triangles, or anything you like.

PINCUSHION

You do not need a pincushion in order to sew, but one would come in handy. Picking pins out of a box is hard work. Picking pins out of a pincushion is easy.

A fine pincushion can be made from a scrap of felt or any sturdy fabric which is at least 4 inches wide and 8 inches long, and no larger than 5 inches by 10 inches.

Follow the directions for making a square pillow. Of course, pincushions do not have to be square. Like pillows, they can be made in many shapes.

POTHOLDER

Sew a new cover for an old potholder.

TYPE OF FABRIC	Use 100 percent cotton percale, gingham, calico, muslin, or denim. *Do not* use man-made fibers such as Dacron or polyester for potholders. Touching a hot pot could melt fabric made from man-made fibers.
SIZE OF FABRIC	1 inch wider than the old potholder and twice as long plus 1 inch
YARN	4 or 5 arm lengths
STUFFING	An old but clean potholder

Cutting the Fabric

Measure the old potholder. Fold the fabric in half so that it forms two layers. Pin the layers together. Measure and mark the fabric 1/2 inch wider than the potholder on each side. Cut on the marked lines through both layers of fabric.

Sewing the Potholder Together

Pin through both layers of fabric on three sides. The pins should be about 1/4 inch from the edge. Leave one end open. Slip the old potholder between the layers, then pin the open end closed.

Sew all the way around the potholder with blanket stitches. Be sure the stitches are 1/2 inch deep so that the needle and yarn go through the old potholder. This will keep it from curling up inside the new cover.

Making a Loop

To make a loop for hanging the potholder, cut three pieces of yarn each 3 inches long. Pin them, one on top of the other, to one corner of the potholder. Thread a darning needle with the same yarn and tack them securely.

Braid the three strands together by crossing the right-hand strand over the middle (a), then the left-hand strand over the middle (b), and repeating till the braid is complete. Tack the end of the braid to the opposite side of the same corner of the potholder.

a

b

SWEATBAND

TYPE OF FABRIC | An old terry cloth bath or hand towel; an old pillowcase, or the end of a sheet; or muslin, percale, or broadcloth

SIZE OF FABRIC | 4 inches by 24 inches if you are using terry cloth; 8 inches by 24 inches if you are using lightweight cotton fabric (which does not absorb as much perspiration as terry cloth)

YARN | 2 or 3 arm lengths

NOTIONS | A piece of 1/2-inch to 1-inch-wide elastic which is 2 inches long

Cutting the Fabric

Measure and mark the fabric using a ruler and chalk. It may be difficult to follow thread lines on terry cloth. If so, use the edges of the towel as a guide.

Sewing the Sweatband Together

Fold the short ends back 1 inch toward the wrong side. Pin in place. Sew with running stitches. Remove the pins.

Fold the long sides back 3/4 inch toward the wrong side. Pin in place.

If you are using terry cloth, fold one of the long sides back again until it almost meets the folded edge of the opposite long side. Pin in place. If you are using thinner fabric, fold it in half twice before pinning in place.

Sew the long sides together using running stitches. Try not to sew all the way through to the opposite side of the sweatband; sew through about three layers of fabric.

Slip 1 inch of elastic between the folds at one end and pin in place. Making sure the sweatband is not twisted, slip the other end of the elastic between the folds of the other end of the sweatband and pin in place. Stitch the ends of the elastic to the sweatband with two or three tack stitches on each side.

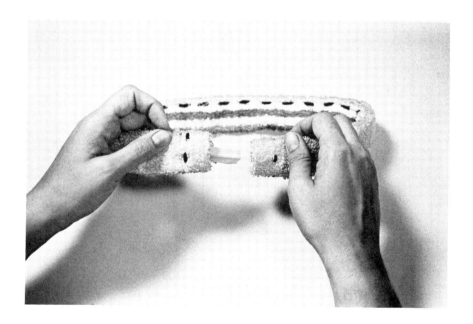

DRAWSTRING BAG

TYPE OF FABRIC	Felt, denim, muslin, gingham, or a sturdy printed cotton; wool or wool blends which match a skirt or pants
SIZE OF FABRIC	Suggested: 12 inches by 16 inches, but it can be as small as 8 inches by 16 inches, and as large as 16 inches by 24 inches
YARN	4 or 5 arm lengths for the suggested size; additional decoration or a larger bag will need more yarn
NOTIONS	A cotton or leather shoelace, 18 inches long; medium-sized safety pin

Cutting the Fabric

A 12-by-16-inch piece of fabric makes a bag 8 inches long and 12 inches wide. Measure and mark your fabric with chalk following lengthwise and crosswise threads. Cut carefully along the chalk lines.

Sewing the Bag Together

Fold back one of the long sides of fabric 2 inches toward the right side. Pin in place. Sew with backstitches about 3/4 inch from the folded edge. This forms a casing or tube for the drawstring to run through.

Pull threads from the cut edge below the backstitching until you have a fringe 1/2 inch deep.

Fold the bag in half so that the short sides meet exactly. Pin in place. Also pin the bottom edges together. Leave the ends of the casing open above the stitching.

Sew around the pinned sides about 3/4 inch inside the edges, using backstitches. All tacks and knots should be on the wrong side. Remove the pins.

Fringe the sides and bottom of the bag 1/2 inch deep.

Pulling the Drawstring Through the Casing

Attach one end of the shoelace to the safety pin. Close the pin. Push the pin through the casing by working the fabric with your fingers from the outside. Push the fabric from the front end of the safety

pin to the back end. When the pin comes out the far end of the casing, adjust the shoelace so that an equal length hangs from each end. Remove the safety pin. Gather the casing together so that the open end of the bag is shut. Tie the shoelace in a bow or knot.

APRONS

Chef's Apron

TYPE OF FABRIC   Unbleached, bleached, or colored muslin; checked or plaid gingham; denim

SIZE OF FABRIC	22 inches by 44 inches
YARN	8 or 9 arm lengths
NOTIONS	2 yards of 1-inch twill tape (optional)

Cutting the Fabric

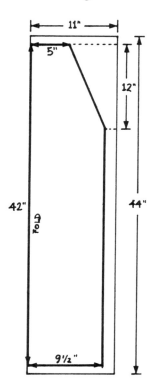

Fold the fabric in half so that it forms two layers 11 inches by 44 inches. Pin the layers together at the corners and every 3 or 4 inches along the edges.

Measure and mark the apron with a ruler and chalk as shown.

Cut on the chalk lines through both layers of fabric. Unfold the apron and lay it flat on the cutting table.

If you don't have twill tape, save the fabric which is left over after you have cut out the apron for making straps and ties. Or use a contrasting fabric for the straps and ties.

Sewing the Apron

Fold back the bottom of the apron 1/2 inch toward the right side. Pin in place. Sew near the folded edge with running stitches. Fold back the same side again 9 inches toward the right side. Pin in place.

This forms a large pocket.

Fold back one of the long sides 1/4 inch toward the wrong side. Crease the fold with your thumbnail. Turn the same side back another 1/4 inch and pin in place. Pin the other unfinished sides the same way. Sew all the folded sides with running stitches. Remove the pins.

Divide the large pocket into several smaller pockets by sewing two seams from the bottom of the pocket to the top, as shown. Use running stitches or backstitches to make strong seams.

Making Straps and Ties

Cut two lengths of twill tape each 27 inches long. Cut a third length 18 inches long.

Or measure and mark with chalk two lengths of fabric 2 inches wide and 27 inches long. Mark a third length 2 inches wide and 18 inches long. Fold the long edges back toward the wrong side 1/4 inch. Bring folded edges together. Pin in place. Sew together with running stitches.

Fold back one end of each 27-inch tie 1/4 inch. Fold them each back again 1/4 inch. Pin one folded end to each side of the apron. Fold back the ends of the 18-inch length and pin to the top of the apron. Sew the strap and ties to the apron with tack stitches.

Carpenter's Apron

TYPE OF FABRIC	Heavy denim or muslin
SIZE OF FABRIC	22 inches by 35 inches
YARN	7 or 8 arm lengths
NOTIONS	2 yards of 1-inch twill tape (optional)

Follow the directions for making a chef's apron, but cut it only 35 inches long. Adjust the width of the pockets to fit whatever tools are to be stored in them. Use backstitches to make strong seams.

MAKING PATTERNS FOR PROJECTS

The projects which follow are started by making a paper pattern. Then the pattern is pinned on top of the fabric and the fabric is cut around the edge of the pattern. You will need large grocery bags, paper scissors, and a felt-tipped pen, a crayon, or a soft lead pencil to make patterns.

Drawing a Pattern

Cut open a grocery bag and lay it flat on the cutting table. Remove the bottom section and throw it away.

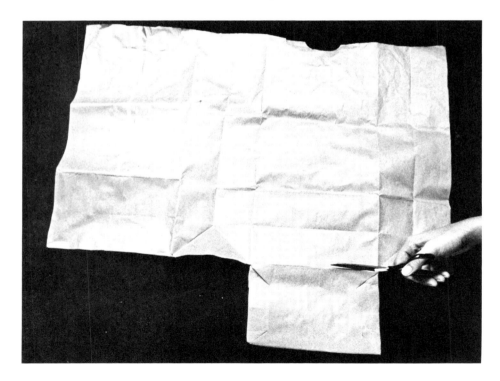

Fold the remaining piece along one of the creased edges.

Measure and draw the pattern following the directions for the project you are making. Draw half the pattern on the top half of the folded bag. Draw lightly until you have the outline the way you want it to look. Then go over the outline with a darker line, using pencil, felt-tipped pen, or sharp crayon. Cut around the outline through *both* layers of the bag. Unfold the bag. Your pattern is ready to use.

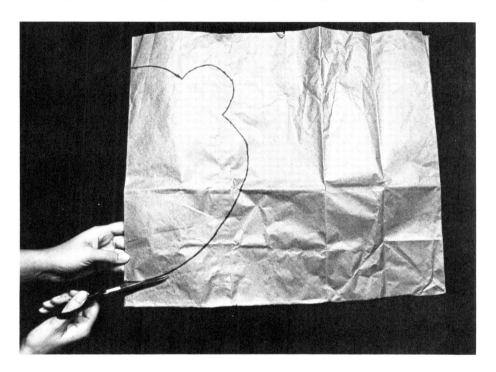

Pinning the Pattern to Fabric

When you place a pattern on fabric, pay attention to the direction of the threads. Be sure your pattern lines up with the grain of the fabric. The center fold should line up with a lengthwise or crosswise thread.

Pins should be spaced about 2 inches apart all the way around the pattern. They should be about 1/2 inch inside the edges. Make sure the pins go through all the layers.

Cutting Around the Pattern

Place one hand on the pattern to hold it and the fabric flat on the table. Holding your shears in the other hand, cut through the fabric all the way around the pattern. If you are right-handed, cut with the pattern to the left of your shears so you can see where you are cutting. If you are left-handed, cut with the pattern to the right of your shears.

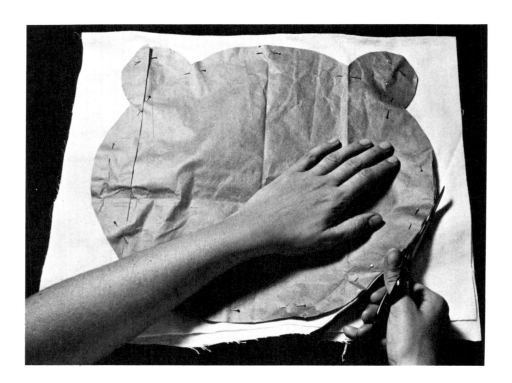

After cutting, remove the pins and separate the pattern from the fabric. Write the name of the project on the pattern. Put it in a box labeled "Patterns for Yarn Sewing" and store the box in the drawer or closet where you keep sewing materials.

ANIMAL PILLOWS

Lion Cub Pillow

TYPE OF FABRIC	Muslin, denim, chintz, cotton flannel, felt, or sturdy cotton print
SIZE OF FABRIC	14 inches by 28 inches
YARN	9 to 12 arm lengths of main color; 2 to 3 arm lengths of each of two contrasting colors
LARGE GROCERY BAG	
STUFFING	See page 9 for suggestions

Making the Pattern

Cut a piece from the grocery bag 14 inches long and 14 inches wide. Fold it in half so that it forms two layers 7 inches by 14 inches. Draw one-half of the lion cub's head on one-half of the paper pattern. Cut around the drawing through both layers of paper. Unfold the pattern and press it flat with your hand.

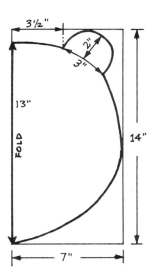

Cutting the Fabric

Fold the fabric in half so that it forms two layers 14 inches by 14 inches. Place the pattern on the fabric so that the crease in the paper lines up with one of the threads in the fabric. Pin the pattern through both layers of fabric. Cut around the pattern through both layers. Remove the pins. One of the pieces you have cut is the front of the pillow. The other is the back.

Making the Lion Cub's Face

Put the back piece of the pillow aside. Place the front piece on the cutting table so that the right side faces up.

Draw the eyes, nose, and other features with chalk. To make sure the parts of the face are in the right positions, you can make guidelines. Fold the front piece in half so one side is directly over the other, and mark the fold line with chalk. The nose and mouth should be centered on the line, and the eyes should be about 2 inches from the line on each side. Make the top of the nose about halfway between the top and bottom of the face, with the eyes just above, as shown. To make round eyes and nose, place one end of a thread spool on the fabric and draw around it.

To sew the face, follow the chalk lines with backstitches. Stitches should be about 1/4 inch long.

You may want to use yarn of one color for the eyes, nose and mouth, and yarn of another color for the whiskers. Use tack stitches for the centers of the eyes.

Sewing the Pillow Together

Place the front of the pillow exactly on top of the back piece so that the right sides of both pieces face out and the wrong sides face each other. All edges should match. Pin the ears together first, placing the pins at least 1 inch away from the edges. Pin the rest of the head together. Measure 1/2 inch from the edge all the way around and mark with chalk.

The lion cub in the photograph is sewn with backstitches around the head, with blanket stitches added around the ears. Unless you are using felt, the edges should be folded under to keep them from unraveling. Make cuts in the fabric on both sides of each ear, as shown. These cuts should be about 1/2 inch long. Fold the edges of the head in toward the wrong side along the chalked lines all the way around, *except* around the ears. Pin all the folded edges in place. The

easiest way to do this is to pin one small section at a time. Place your pins as close to the folded edges as you can. Be sure to pin through all layers of fabric.

Sew the front and back pieces together with backstitches. Stitch about 1/4 inch in from the folded edges. Leave about 4 inches open at the bottom of the pillow to add the stuffing. Sew around the ears with blanket stitches. You may add a line of backstitches at the inside of the blanket stitches in the same or a different color.

If the lion cub's ears are stuffed, they will stand up straight. If you do not want to stuff the ears, mark lines between the ears and the head. Backstitch on the lines. This makes floppy ears.

Be sure all knots and tacks are on the back side of the pillow, or between the folds.

Stuffing the Pillow

Stuff the top of the head first, and work your way toward the bottom. Pack the stuffing a bit loosely. Sew the bottom together with the same stitch you used around the edges.

Owl Pillow

TYPE OF FABRIC	Muslin, denim, chintz, cotton flannel, felt, or sturdy cotton print
SIZE OF FABRIC	24 inches by 13 inches for the body; contrasting fabric 3 inches by 9 inches for the face; scraps for eyes
YARN	9 to 12 arm lengths of main color, 2 to 3 arm lengths of each of two contrasting colors
LARGE GROCERY BAG	
STUFFING	See page 9 for suggestions

Making the Pattern

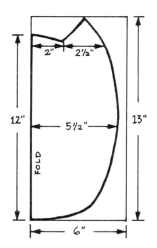

Following directions for the lion cub, draw and cut out the pattern for the owl. Pin the pattern to the fabric and cut out the two pieces of the owl pillow. Remove the pattern.

Making the Owl's Breast and Face

Find the center line of the front piece by folding it in half so one side is directly over the other. Mark the fold line with chalk. Draw a triangle with the tip about 5 inches up from the bottom, and add slanted lines about 1/2 inch apart as shown. Sew on the lines with large backstitches, each about 1/2 inch long.

To make a paper pattern for the face, draw around a small bowl or coaster on a piece of paper. Make two circles and connect them

50

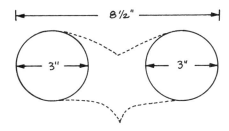

as shown in the diagram. Cut around the drawing. Pin it to the contrasting fabric. Cut around the pattern and remove it. Using large and small spools as guides, cut two large circles and two small ones for eyes.

Pin the face on just above the triangle and sew it on with running stitches about 1/2 inch long. Pin eye circles about 2 inches on either side of the center line and attach with tack stitches.

Sewing the Pillow Together

Pin the two pieces together all the way around. After matching all the edges as well as you can, you may still see places where they do not meet exactly. Trim these places with your shears. Make a chalk line 1/2 inch inside the raw edge.

You may backstitch on the chalk line and then sew with blanket stitches, or you may use blanket stitches alone, with the chalk line as a guide. The owl in the photograph is sewed together with backstitches and blanket stitches. Leave about 4 inches open at the bottom of the pillow to add the stuffing.

Stuffing the Pillow

Follow the directions for stuffing the lion cub pillow and closing the opening.

Dog Pillow

TYPE OF FABRIC	Muslin, denim, chintz, cotton flannel, felt, or sturdy cotton print
SIZE OF FABRIC	14 inches by 19 inches; scraps of contrasting fabric for face, ears, and tail
YARN	9 to 12 arm lengths of main color; 2 to 3 arm lengths of contrasting color
PIECE OF GROCERY BAG	
STUFFING	See page 9 for suggestions

Making the Patterns

You will not need a paper pattern for the dog's body because it is in the shape of a rectangle. You will need patterns, however, for the tail, ears, and nose.

On a piece of a grocery bag, draw an ear, a curved tail, and a nose. Cut out the pattern pieces and label them clearly. Cut out paper circles as patterns for the eyes, using a large thread spool as a guide.

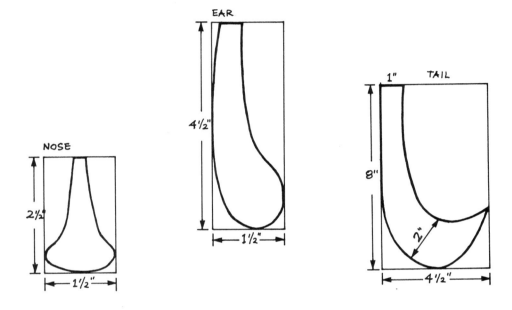

Cutting the Fabric

Measure and mark with a ruler and chalk a piece of fabric 14 inches wide and 19 inches long. Cut around the fabric on the chalk lines.

Using a fabric of contrasting color, pin the patterns for the ears, eyes, and tail on double layers of fabric. Cut around the patterns. Pin the nose pattern on a single layer of fabric and cut around it.

Sewing the Dog's Face, Legs, and Tail

Pin the ears, eyes, and nose on the lower half of the fabric rectangle as shown. The dog's face can be just a little bit crooked if you like.

53

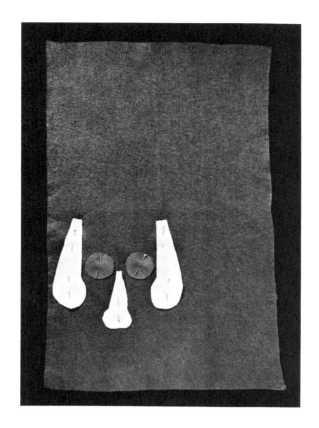

Sew around the ears, eyes, and nose with backstitches. Stitch smaller circles inside the eyes, using a small thread spool as a guide.

Draw a mouth under the nose. Sew it with backstitches.

Also draw both of the dog's front feet and one back leg and foot. Outline them with backstitches.

Sew the two pieces of the tail together with backstitches. Then attach the tail to the body with tack stitches.

Sewing the Pillow Together

Fold the rectangle in half. Pin, stitch, and stuff the dog following the directions for the lion cub.

HALTER

TYPE OF FABRIC	Denim, muslin, chambray; printed, checked, striped, or plaid cotton
SIZE OF FABRIC	36 inches by 36 inches
YARN	4 or 5 arm lengths in either the same color as the fabric or a contrasting color, for the halter; about 2 arm lengths each for the straps
NOTIONS	Medium safety pin
LARGE GROCERY BAG	

Making the Pattern

This halter makes about a junior size 9 or a misses' size 10. By cutting the pattern 1/4 inch smaller on the sides and top, you can make a halter which is smaller than a size 9. By cutting the pattern 1/4 inch larger on the sides and top, you can make a larger halter.

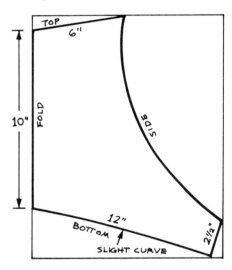

Cut a piece 24 inches by 18 inches from a grocery bag. Fold the piece in half so that it forms two layers 12 inches by 18 inches. Draw one-half of the halter shape on one side of the paper pattern. Measure and mark lightly with a soft pencil. When you are sure the pencil lines are in the right positions, go over them with a heavy line. Cut along the bottom, side, and top through both layers. Do not cut the fold line.

Unfold the paper pattern. Lay it flat on the cutting table.

Cutting the Fabric

Place the pattern on the fabric as shown in the photograph. Instead of lining the pattern up with the lengthwise threads, place it diagonally to the threads. This is called cutting on the bias. It will make the halter fit comfortably around the chest and back without binding.

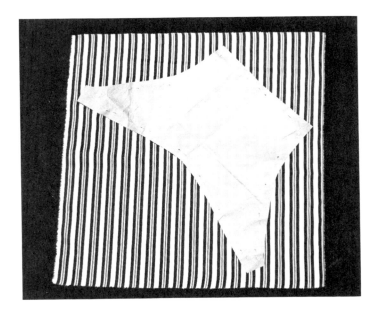

To find the diagonal, start with a square piece of fabric. Draw a chalk line from the top left corner to the bottom right corner. Place the center fold of the pattern on this line.

Pin the pattern in place. Cut around bottom, sides, and top. Remove the pins and the pattern.

On the fabric which is left over, measure two strips 36 inches long and 1-1/2 inches wide. Mark them with chalk. Cut carefully along the chalk lines. These pieces will be made into straps to tie around the neck and back.

Sewing the Halter

Turn back the edge of one side 1/4 inch toward the wrong side. Crease the folded edge with your thumbnail. Turn back the folded edge another 1/4 inch and pin in place. Sew it with running stitches. Repeat this with the other side.

Turn back the edge of the top 1/2 inch toward the wrong side. Turn the folded edge back another 1/2 inch toward the wrong side and pin in place. Sew it with running stitches as shown.

Next, turn back and stitch the bottom edge the same way as you did the top.

The top and bottom are now narrow tubes or casings through which the straps will be pulled.

Making the Straps

Fold the short ends of one of the straps back 1/4 inch toward the wrong side. Crease the fold with your thumbnail. Fold the long ends back 1/4 inch toward the wrong side. Crease the folds with your thumbnail. Fold the strap in half so that the long folded sides meet exactly. Pin the edges together carefully. Sew with running stitches.

Repeat these steps to make the second strap.

Pulling the Straps Through the Casings

Attach a medium-sized safety pin to the end of one of the straps. Follow directions on page 36 for pulling a drawstring through a casing. Repeat this with the second strap.

Wearing the Halter

To wear the halter, tie the ends of the top strap together at the back of your neck. Tie the ends of the bottom strap together under your shoulder blades. Adjust the gathers at the neck and stomach.

EYE MASK

TYPE OF FABRIC	Felt, cotton flannel, muslin, denim
SIZE OF FABRIC	7 inches by 7 inches
YARN	3 or 4 arm lengths
NOTIONS	Elastic, 12 to 15 inches long, 1 inch wide
SMALL GROCERY BAG	

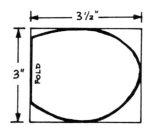

Making the Pattern

Cut a piece 7 inches by 3 inches from the grocery bag. Fold it in half so that it forms two layers 3-1/2 inches by 3 inches. Draw one-half of the eye mask as shown. Cut around the pattern through both layers. Hold it up to your eyes to make sure the mask fits your face. Ask someone to check the position of your eyes. Mark carefully with chalk where one of the eye holes should be. Cut the hole out.

Fold the pattern in half. Draw around the inside of the first eye hole. This will mark the second hole on the other side of the pattern. Make any needed changes in the position of these holes before cutting them out. Hold the pattern up to your eyes again after cutting. If you can't see well through the holes, cut them larger.

You can also cut eye holes by folding the pattern in half and cutting through both layers of paper at the same time.

Cutting the Fabric

Fold the fabric in half so that it forms two layers 3-1/2 inches by 7 inches. Pin the pattern on the fabric. Cut around the pattern. To cut out the eye holes, pinch the fabric together at the center of the eye hole to start the cut, then cut toward one edge of the eye hole. Continue cutting around the edge. Remove the pattern.

Sewing the Mask

Pin the two pieces of the mask together, matching the edges exactly. Sew around the outside edge with blanket stitches.

Sew around the eye holes with blanket stitches.

Pin the elastic to the back of the mask. Be sure the elastic is pinned near the top edge of the mask. Try it on to check the fit. You may need to shorten the elastic so that the mask feels comfortable.

Sew the elastic to the mask with tack stitches.

HOODED MASK

TYPE OF FABRIC	Soft but closely woven cotton such as percale, fine broadcloth, or flannel; lightweight muslin
SIZE OF FABRIC	18 inches by 28 inches
YARN	6 or 7 arm lengths of one color for sewing the hood together; 3 arm lengths of a second color for stitching around the eyes and nose; 1 arm length of a third color for stitching around the mouth and for making freckles, warts, scars, or other improvements

LARGE GROCERY BAG

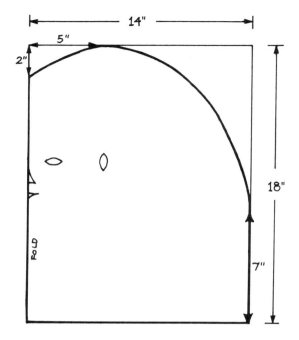

Making the Pattern

Cut a piece 14 inches by 18 inches from the grocery bag. Draw one-half of the mask on the paper as shown. Draw ear, eye, nose, and mouth holes on the pattern. The eye should be about 5 inches from the top of the front edge and about 1 inch in from the edge. The mouth should be about 7 inches up from the bottom. The ear should start 5 inches from the edge.

Cut around the pattern. Cut out the holes for the eye, ear, nose, and mouth.

Cutting the Fabric

Fold the fabric in half so that it forms two layers 14 inches by 18 inches. Place the pattern on the fabric. Pin the pattern through both layers of fabric. Cut around the pattern through these two layers. Mark the eyes, nose, mouth, and ears with chalk on one side. *Do not cut out the holes.* Remove the paper pattern.

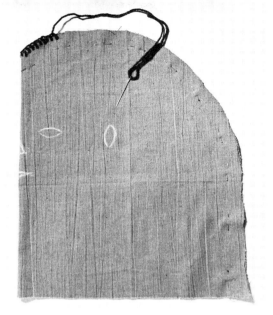

Sewing the Hood Together

Pin the top and back of the hood together with the right sides facing out. Sew with blanket stitches. Remove the pins.

Try the hood on. Ask someone to check the positions of the marks where the holes will be cut for the eyes, ears, nose, and mouth. If they are not in the right positions, ask this person to make new marks with chalk and to brush off the old chalk marks.

Making the Mask Face

Cut out the holes for eyes, ears, nose, and mouth.

Try the hood on again. Check the position of each hole. Your ears should stick out through the ear holes. You must be able to see through the eye holes and to breathe through the nose hole. You may find you must cut the holes a bit larger.

Sew around each hole with blanket stitches. To add eyebrows use backstitches. Round red cheeks may also be added with backstitches. Freckles, scars, warts, or other spots and lines may be made with tack stitches, backstitches, or blanket stitches.

Finish the hood by turning back the bottom edge 1/2 inch and sewing with running stitches.

STOCKING CAP

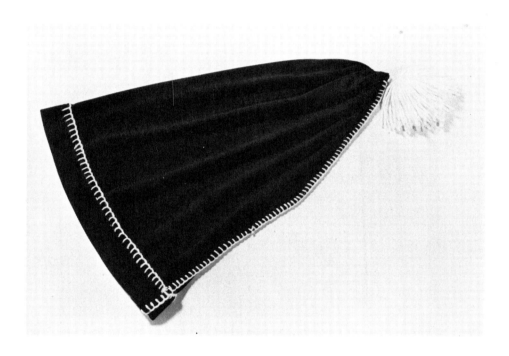

TYPE OF FABRIC	Knit fabric (cotton, wool, man-made); the back of a man's old knit shirt is one possibility
SIZE OF FABRIC	24 inches by 20 inches
YARN	9 or 10 arm lengths for sewing cap together; 3 or 4 arm lengths for pompon
LARGE GROCERY BAG	

64

Making the Pattern

Cut a piece 12 inches by 20 inches from the grocery bag. Draw the pattern using measurements as shown. Cut around the pattern.

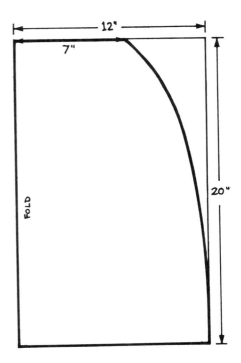

Cutting the Fabric

Knit fabric is best for a stocking cap because it is stretchy and fits the head snugly.

If you look closely at knit fabric, you will see that it is knitted just like a sweater. Lines of stitches run from the top to the bottom.

Fold the fabric in half along one of these long rows of stitches to form two layers of cloth.

Place the pattern on the fabric so that the long, straight side of the pattern is on the fold. Cut around the pattern through both layers of fabric. Remove the pattern.

Sewing the Cap Together

Fold the two curved edges under 1/2 inch toward the wrong side and pin them together. Leave the top and bottom ends open. Sew the curved edges together with blanket stitches. Hide knots and tacks between the layers of fabric.

To make the hem, first turn under 1/2 inch along the bottom edge. Pin it in place. Turn the cap wrong side out. Fold the bottom edge up again toward the wrong side 2-1/2 inches. Pin in place. Fasten this hem with running stitches, each about 1/4 inch long, all the way around. Sew with blanket stitches along the bottom edge of the hem. Be sure to do the blanket stitching from the wrong side, as shown, so that all knots and tacks will be hidden.

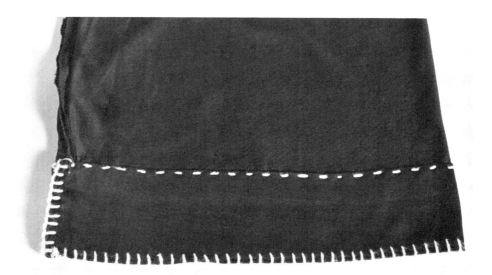

With the cap still wrong side out, close the top by first sewing with running stitches 1/2 inch from the edge. Then pull the yarn to gather the fabric as tightly as possible. Tack the yarn firmly in place.

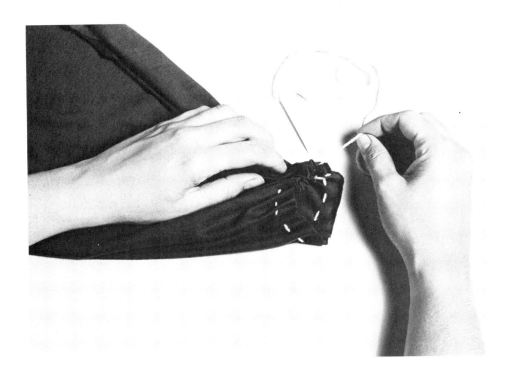

To finish, turn the cap right side out. Fold the bottom edge of the hem up 2 inches toward the right side to form a cuff. Pin the cuff in place. Tack it on the wrong side every 2 inches near the seam of running stitches. Remove the pins.

Making a Pompon

To make a fat pompon for the gathered end of the cap, wrap a length of yarn one hundred times around a piece of cardboard 2 inches wide and 5 inches long. Place a 9-inch length of yarn under the yarn on the cardboard (a). Slide the yarn off the cardboard and tie the 9-inch piece tightly (b). Cut open the loops. Sew the pompon to the end of the cap, pulling the two long pieces of yarn through to the wrong side. Tie them together in a knot three or four times. Snip off the ends.

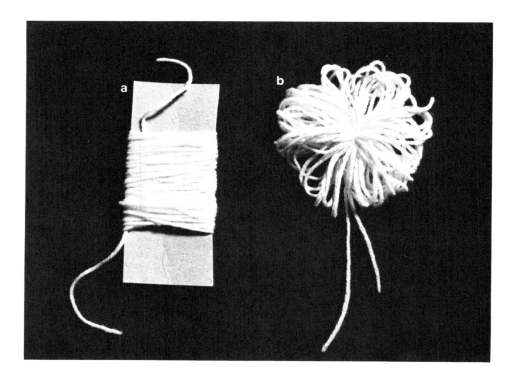

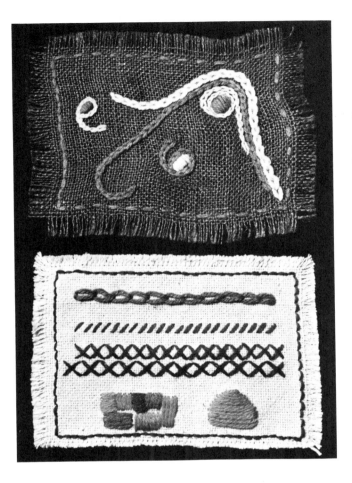

THREE MORE STITCHES

Now that you have learned how to handle a needle and yarn, you are ready to learn a few new stitches. Try chain, satin, and cross stitches in several combinations and sizes on a practice mat.

Chain Stitch

These make interesting single lines, which look like links in a chain. In rows, they are good for filling in spaces. The wall hanging on page 76 has circles filled in with chain stitches.

Mark lines with chalk where chain stitches are to be sewn.

Bring the needle up from the wrong to the right side. Form a loop; hold it with your thumb. Put the needle back down from the right to the wrong side very close to where it came up (a). Bring it back up about 1/4 inch along the line. Pull the yarn all the way through (b). This forms one chain stitch.

Repeat to make a chain of stitches.

a

b

Satin Stitch

This is a filling stitch which makes a smooth, satiny surface. The tree trunk in the wall hanging on page 76 is filled with satin stitches.

Bring the needle up from the wrong to the right side at the left edge of the area to be filled in. Put the needle back down at the opposite edge of the area to be filled in (a). Return to the starting line (b) by carrying the yarn underneath the fabric.

a

b

Stitches should be close together. They can be exactly the same length to form squares or rectangles, or they may be different lengths to fill in leaves, flowers, or other designs.

Cross Stitch

Cross stitches look like crosses. You probably have seen samplers with tiny cross stitches made by children many years ago. But cross stitches can be made large or small.

If you have a piece of checked gingham, you can make cross stitches using the squares as guidelines. If you use plain fabric, measure the squares carefully. Cross stitches should be exactly the same size. They make excellent borders or filling stitches.

Bring your needle up from the wrong to the right side at A. Put the needle back down at B, and back up again at C. After you have made diagonal stitches in one direction, make them in the opposite direction to complete the crosses, finishing from C to D.

MATS AND HANGINGS

Mats and hangings are almost always squares or rectangles. They can be simple or complicated in design. Large table mats and wall hangings take longer to make, of course, than small ones, so it is wise not to try a large mat or hanging with an all-over design until you are experienced at yarn sewing. Later on, you might want to spend several weeks or even months working on an ambitious project.

You can choose from a wide variety of fabrics to make mats and hangings. In fact, you can use just about anything you like. Cottons, from the gauziest curtain material to the heaviest upholstery fabric; wool and linen, and even silk velvet are good choices for mats and hangings. Place mats, however, should be made from strong, washable fabrics such as linen toweling, colorful muslin, denim, gingham, or textured cotton.

Yarns also can vary a great deal. If you like to experiment, a wall hanging is an ideal project for trying metal yarn, twine, raffia, crochet cotton, or rug yarn.

Directions for making a mat and a hanging are included to show you how to go about starting this type of project. But you can use your imagination in endless ways to create your own designs.

Place Mat

TYPE OF FABRIC	Denim, gingham, muslin, heavy textured cotton
SIZE OF FABRIC	12-inch by 16-inch piece for each place mat
YARN	5 arm lengths for border; 9 arm lengths for fork, knife, and spoon

Cutting the Fabric

Measure fabric with a ruler and chalk, following lengthwise and crosswise threads. Cut along chalk lines.

Remove two or three threads all the way around the mat to start the fringe. Trim the edges if they are uneven.

Making the Place Mat

Mark a straight line with chalk 3/4 inch from the edge on each of the four sides of the mat. Sew with backstitches on these lines all the way around.

Sewing the Design

Place a fork, a knife, and a spoon on the place mat in the correct positions. Trace around them with chalk. Remove the silverware.

Sew with backstitches on the chalk lines.

Make a fringe 1/2 inch deep all the way around the edge of the mat.

Wall Hanging

TYPE OF FABRIC	Monk's cloth, denim, unbleached muslin, or a light-colored upholstery fabric
SIZE OF FABRIC	11 inches by 16 inches
YARN	10 to 12 arm lengths of a dark color for the tree trunk; 6 arm lengths of each of three bright colors for the round leaves; 10 to 12 arm lengths of a medium-dark color to outline the tree trunk; 3 arm lengths of one of the leaf colors for the border
WOODEN DOWEL	Two pieces each 12 inches long and 1/4 inch in diameter
CORD	A sturdy piece about 2 feet long
SMALL GROCERY BAG	

76

Cutting the Hanging

Measure and mark fabric with ruler and chalk, following thread lines carefully. Cut along chalk lines.

Pull out two or three threads from the cut edges all the way around. Trim off any uneven edges.

Finishing the Edges

Turn back short ends 1-1/4 inches toward the wrong side. Pin in place. Mark straight lines 3/4 inch from the folded edges of the short sides. Mark lines 1/2 inch from the edges of the long sides. Sew all the way around on the lines with running stitches.

Making the Design

Cut a piece from the grocery bag 10 inches by 13 inches. Draw a tree with two or three branches. Use thread spools of different sizes to draw circles for leaves along the branches and falling toward the base of the trunk.

Cut the circles out first and put them aside. Then cut around the trunk and branches.

Pin the trunk and branches on the right side of the hanging. Arrange the circles on the branches. Pin them in place.

Draw around the paper patterns with chalk or pencil. Remove the patterns.

Sewing the Design

Fill in the trunk and branches with satin stitches. Outline them with backstitches if you wish.

Sew the circles with chain stitches. Stitch around the outer edge of each circle first. Then work toward the center. Space the colors used in the circles around the tree so that each color is used near the top and near the bottom.

Hanging the Hanging

Slip the dowels into the top and bottom casings. Tie the cord to the ends of the top dowel. Then put a thumbtack into a wall and hang the cord from the tack.

GLOSSARY

acrylic   a man-made fiber noted for its quick-drying ability

arm length of yarn   a piece of yarn as long as your arm

bias   the invisible line that runs diagonally from one corner of a woven square of fabric to the opposite corner

bolt   a roll of fabric from 36 inches to 72 inches wide and many yards long

cotton   a fiber from the cotton plant, used to make a wide variety of threads and fabrics

Dacron   the trade name for a polyester fiber

darning needle   a large needle with a sharp point

fibers   natural and man-made strands which are spun into threads used to weave fabric

fabric   material woven or knitted from threads

linen   a fiber that comes from the flax plant, which is woven into fabric known for its strength

linens   tablecloths, towels, sheets, and pillowcases, so called because many years ago most of these articles were woven of linen threads

notions   small sewing equipment such as needles, pins, and thread

nylon   a very strong man-made fiber

Orlon   the trade name for an acrylic fiber

ply   a thread twisted together with other thread to form a bulkier thread or yarn

polyester   a man-made fiber

raw edge   a cut edge of fabric

seam   a line of stitches which holds two or more pieces of fabric together

selvage   the finished edge of a woven fabric

stitch   a single loop of thread made in fabric by a needle

straight grain of fabric   the direction of lengthwise threads

tapestry yarn   a smooth woolen yarn used in needlepoint

thread   a long strand of spun fiber used to weave fabrics and to sew fabrics together

weave   the process of joining threads to form a fabric

wool   a natural fiber which comes from the fleece of sheep

yarn   several threads twisted together to form a bulky thread